Landscapes of
PAXOS

a countryside guide
Third edition

Noel Rochford

SUNFLOWER BOOKS

Third edition © 2005
Sunflower Books™
PO Box 36160
London SW7 3WS, UK
www.sunflowerbooks.co.uk

Published in the USA by
Hunter Publishing Inc
130 Campus Drive
Edison, NJ 08818
www.hunterpublishing.com

ISBN 1-85691-271-X

Olive press at Fontana/Platanos

Important note to the reader

We have tried to ensure that the descriptions and maps in this book
are error-free at press date. The book will be updated, where
necessary, whenever future printings permit. It will be very helpful
for us to receive your comments (sent in care of the publishers,
please) for the updating of future printings.

   We also rely on those who use this book — especially walkers
— to take along a good supply of common sense when they
explore. Conditions change fairly rapidly on Paxos, and *storm
damage may make a route unsafe at any time*. If the route is not as
we outline it here, and your way ahead is not secure, return to the
point of departure. *Never attempt to complete a tour or walk
under hazardous conditions!* Please read carefully the country
code on page 12, the walking notes on pages 22 and 25, and the
introductory comments at the beginning of each tour and walk
(regarding road conditions, equipment, grade, distances and time,
etc). Explore *safely*, while at the same time respecting the beauty of
the countryside.

Cover photograph: Tripitos Arch (Walk 1)
Photographs: Noel Rochford; cover photograph: Mike Longridge
Maps: John Underwood, based on the Road Editions map of Paxos
   (with permission), but greatly amended and updated
Drawings by Sharon Rochford
A CIP catalogue record for this book is available from the British
   Library.
Printed and bound in Spain by Grafo Industrias Gráficas, Basauri

10 9 8 7 6 5 4 3 2 1

● Preface _____

Preface

Paxos, just 19 sq km of cosy countryside, is little more than a broken fragment of hills sitting anchored off the southern end of Corfu. The hills of Paxos are cloaked in a cool mantle of olive trees. Dark groves of cypresses pierce this silvery-green mantle. In the shade of these wooded hills lie sprinklings of rustic hamlets. But the real beauty of Paxos is the dazzling necklace of turquoise-green coves that collar the eastern coastline.

The moment you step foot on this island you can feel that your stay here is going to be both peaceful and restful. The sleepy fishing villages and the timeless countryside have cast their spell upon you.

You begin to notice just how small the island is when you keep bumping into the same people on your daily jaunts. This creates a certain friendliness amongst the tourists themselves — a friendliness that is further enhanced by the warmth of the islanders. It was this 'neighbourhood' atmosphere that outshone, for me, all the other pleasures of my time on the island.

On Paxos everything is accessible — either a few minutes by public transport, or an hour or two on foot. Outside July and August, when there is little traffic on the island and a freshness in the air, the charm of the countryside draws you out into it — usually on foot. Everyone seems to go out for a stroll.

Here's where *Landscapes of Paxos* will come in handy. There are a number of well-known beauty spots to be seen, and this book leads you to them ... and to other, more hidden corners that most visitors miss.

Being just that little bit out of the way, Paxos up until now has remained free of those obscene multi-storey apartment buildings and hotels that so badly scar the face of many tourist centres. But *do remember* that during July and August Paxos does become very crowded. Most of the visitors, fortunately, are only day-trippers from Corfu ... we have the mornings and evenings to ourselves.

Happy holiday.

Acknowledgements

Thanks to my sister, Sharon, for her splendid drawings, but most especially, thanks to Mike Longridge for his thorough revision of this third edition.

Mike, in turn, would like to thank Thomas Arvanitakis and Marianthi of Arvanitakis Travel in Gaios for advice, information and assistance — as well as David and Jean Cavill, summer residents of Paxos, who enlivened the car tour with their anecdotes, local knowledge, and good company.

Loggos — as perfect as a picture postcard

Recommended map and books

Bleasdale Walking Map of Paxos, 9th edition, 2004. At a scale of 1:10,000, this shows every path on Paxos (and more besides)! A labour of love; for the enthusiast; widely available on the island.

Poulin, O and Huxley, A: *Flowers of the Mediterranean.* London, Chatto & Windus.

Sfikis, G: *Wild Flowers of Greece; Trees and Shrubs of Greece; Medicinal Plants of Greece.* Athens, Efstathiadis.

Photographs and drawings of island flora

Acanthus spinosus 21; *Agave americana* 51; *Amaryllis belladonna* 36-37; *Anacamptis pyramidalis* 53; Anemone 53; *Cercis siliquastrum* 21; Cyclamen 39; *Cupressus sempervirens* 40-41; *Erica arborea* 49; *Euphorbia dendroides* 39; *Juniperus oxycedrus* 39; *Nicotiana glauca* 11; *Phlomis fruticosa* 11; *Pistacia lentiscus* 11; *Punica granatum* 11; Ranunculus 53; *Sarcopoterium spinosum* 11; Senecio 39; Sternbergia 21, 50; *Urginea maritima* 53; *Vitex agnuscastus* 39

GAIOS KEY

1	Main square	7	Taxi boats to Antipaxos, Moggonissi, etc	12	Bakery
2	Bus			13	Pharmacy
3	Post office	8	Ferry tickets	14	Scooter rental
4	Telephones	9	Police	15	Parking
5	Taxis	10	Doctor	16	Supermarket
6	Ferry dock	11	Dentist	3→	Starting points for walks (1-4)

● Transport

Paxos is so small (19 square kilometres) that one can get around quite easily using the fairly regular **bus service**. If you are staying at one of the many secluded tourist villas, and you have children with you, then a hired **car** is advisable. Cars can be hired through your tour company or directly from the agency in Gaios. **Mopeds** and **motorbikes** are widely available for hire. And there's also the appealing option of hiring an outboard **motorboat**, to reach the many otherwise inaccessible coves and beaches that dot the shoreline. Finally you have the option of hiring a **taxi**, and the prices are very reasonable. Check the price before setting out, however, and don't be afraid to bargain politely if you think you're being taken for a ride metaphorically. Most people, however, get about simply by strolling. And what better place for it?

BUS TIMETABLE

Gaios	Loggos	Lakka	Lakka	Loggos	Gaios
			09.15	09.25	09.45
10.00	10.20	10.30	10.45	*	11.15
11.30	11.50	12.00	12.15	12.25	12.45
13.30	13.50	14.00	14.15	*	14.40
17.30	17.50	18.00	18.15	18.25	18.45

* Not via Loggos. Buses run daily except Sundays and holidays.

FERRY AND HYDROFOIL SERVICES

Two **car and passenger ferries** operate five services weekly between Corfu, Paxos and Igoumenitsa: Corfu to Paxos via Igoumenitsa takes approximately 3-5 hours. These vessels leave Corfu from the New Port and dock at Gaios New Port.

The two **hydrofoils**, Santa II and Santa III, operated by Petrakis Lines, are faster (1h10min) and direct. There are up to three services daily during the main season (May to mid-October), but fewer in spring and autumn. Tickets to Paxos can be purchased at the Petrakis Lines office outside the entrance to the New Port in Corfu Town.

It is best to confirm all ferry and hydrofoil times a day or two ahead of your sailing.

☀ Picnicking _____

Who needs an excuse for picnicking on this island, when there are so many out-of-the-way coves to explore? All of them offer ideal swimming conditions and all the solitude you could possibly ask for, in addition to a sylvan backdrop which provides the much-needed shade on a hot day.

There's only one picnic spot amongst the suggestions that follow where you will find tables and benches — Picnic 5 at Ag Apostoli. The rest of the settings I recommend are natural, untouched beauty spots. Some are at exhilarating viewpoints, others are in rustic countryside surroundings, but most of them are at beaches, since that's where you're likely to be heading.

Note that picnic numbers correspond to walk numbers: the location of the picnic spot is shown on the map, by the symbol **P**. Please remember to **wear sensible shoes and take a sunhat** (the symbol ○ after the title indicates a picnic **in full sun**. It's a good idea to take along a plastic groundsheet as well, in case its damp or prickly.

1a MOGGONISSI INLET (photograph opposite) ○

🚗 by car: park near the church of Ag Marina at the end of the Moggonissi road; then 15-20 minutes on foot
🚌 by bus: to Gaios only; then 50-55 minutes on foot, at first along the motor road
From the parking area near the church of Ag Marina, follow the lane shown on the facing page. It is now mostly concreted and leads round to the causeway and over to the taverna and beach. But don't cross the causeway; instead, keep along the shoreline and climb the western sea-cliffs, to sit on the magnificent limestone shelves that create an amphitheatre in the face of the cliff. No shade. This would be a wonderful place for an evening picnic, watching the sun go down.

1b MOUZMOULI BAY OVERLOOK (photograph page 17)

🚗 by car: park by the church in Vellianitatika; then 20-30 minutes on foot
🚌 by bus: alight at the taverna just above the Ozias turn-off; then 25-30 minutes on foot
If you're travelling by bus, use the notes for Walk 1 (page 26) to reach this lookout. If you go by car, from Vellianitatika head behind the church and down past the campanile, where you meet a junction. Turn right, then refer to the second paragraph on page 28:

'Once through the houses ...'. This is a very impressive viewpoint; shade nearby.

2a GALAZIO BAY OVERLOOK (photograph page 32)

🚗 by car: park by the church in Vellianitatika; then 20-25 minutes on foot.
🚌 by bus: alight at the taverna just above the Ozias turn-off; then 20-25 minutes on foot

On route to Picnic 1a, we leave the car at the end of the Moggonissi road, near the 6th-century church of Ag Marina, and follow the lane heading round to the causeway.

If travelling by bus, follow the notes for Walk 2 (page 32) to reach this stupendous viewpoint straight across the bay. By car, refer to the 15min-point on page 32: 'Continue past the church …' Shade of trees nearby.

2b AGRILAS BEACH (photograph page 32) ○

🚗 by car: park off the side of the road at Makratika; then 20-30 minutes on foot
🚌 by bus: alight at Makratika; then 20-30 minutes on foot
Following the notes for Walk 2 in the second paragraph on page 34, set out from the church (Il Conde/Pantocratoras, with its noteworthy campanile) in Makratika to descend to Agrilas Beach. Swimming in the inlet is safe, but there is no shade.

3 GEROMONACHES (photograph page 38)

🚗 by car: park at the entrance to the concrete lane that turns off into Klonatika — the first lane off to your right, as you are descending northeast from Bogdanatika towards the New Port road; then 20-30 minutes on foot
🚌 by bus: alight at Bogdanatika, at the New Port road junction; then 20-30 minutes on foot
Follow the route for Walk 3 as shown on the map; this is very straightforward. Take the first lane turning off to the right along the New Port road (motorists park here); then, six minutes later, branch off left into an alley that descends to the derelict hamlet of Geromonaches, one of my favourite settings on Paxos — cool, shady, and timeless.

4 KIPOS BEACH

🚗 by car: park above Kipos Beach; then 10-15 minutes on foot
🚌 by bus: alight at the Koutsi turn-off; then 20-30 minutes on foot
To get there by car or on foot: Approaching from Loggos, take the road turning off left some 100m/yds above the Koutsi turn-off. (Several signposts for villas mark the entrance to the lane.) Remain along the lane, through a junction and over a crest; then bear right at the fork near the end of the lane, above the beach. This is a very pleasant, secluded spot, and there is shade from olive trees.

5 AG APOSTOLI (photographs pages 22-23 and 45)

🚗 by car: park at the end of the lane to Ag Apostoli (turn off in Magazia — the way is well signposted); then 5 minutes on foot
🚌 by bus: alight at the junction of the Ag Apostoli road at Magazia; then 20-30 minutes on foot
This is an excellent setting in the shade of cypress trees, with a picnic table and benches. From the churchyard balcony, you have a splendid view of the Erimitis Cliffs bursting up out of the sea.

6 ABOVE LOGGOS (photograph page 52)

🚗 by car: park in Loggos; then 25-30 minutes on foot
🚌 by bus: alight in Loggos; then 25-30 minutes on foot
Follow the notes at the start of Walk 6 (page 48) to explore the promontory above Loggos. A beautiful panorama over the limestone-trimmed coastline lies barely a minute beyond the first mill. Under the shade of olive trees, one could sit all day and admire the seascape. More intimate coves, all offering plenty of shade, can be reached in a further ten minutes (see walk notes), but

*the descents are steep and not recom-
mended if there are young children in your
party.*

7a CAPE (AKR) LAKKA
(photographs pages 20 and 56-57)

🚗 by car: park in Lakka; then 20-30 minutes
on foot
🚌 by bus: alight in Lakka; then 20-30
minutes on foot
*Using the notes for the beginning of Walk 7
(page 54), picnic anywhere beyond the
second beach. From the top of the headland
crest you have stunning views embracing
the harbour and inland hills shown on page
20. Some shade is on offer. You could also
visit the relatively unfrequented beach on
the north side of the promontory (Missorachi; photograph pages 56-57), where it is
safe to swim, and there is shade from the
cliffs.*

Pistacia lentiscus

*Phlomis fruticosa
(Jerusalem sage)*

7b IPAPANTI CHURCH
(photographs pages 16 and 47)

🚗 by car: Coming from Lakka, turn right
after 1km on a concrete lane. Just over
0.5km along turn right on a narrower lane
and follow signs to the church. This lane
ends after a couple of hundred metres
(parking space for a couple of cars). Allow
5-10 minutes on foot to the church.
🚌 to Lakka only; then 30-40 minutes on
foot (follow the notes for motorists above)
*The church sits at the end of a path off the
lane into the village. You can picnic on the
walls below the grand campanile. This is a
very peaceful spot, with ample shade.*

*Punica granatum
(Pomegranate)*

8 ANTIPAXOS (photograph pages 58-59)

⛴ by taxi boat; 10-20 minutes on foot
*Leave the speedboat at Vrika and follow the
track out. Take the first turn-off to the left (a
path, one minute uphill). This path leads
down to a lovely small cove called Messovrika. There is no immediate shade on the
beach. Most people continue to Voutoumi
Beach — the real beauty spot — so it is
likely to be crowded in high season. If you
want to visit Voutoumi, you can easily get
there by taking the track inland from Vrika.
Follow it round to the left at the top and then
downhill around the headland. At the
bottom turn left to Voutoumi. Bella Vista bar
has a wonderful view from the hillside overlooking the beach, with shade nearby. But it
can still be very hot.*

*Sarcopoterium
spinosum
(Thorny burnet)*

*Nicotiana glauca
(Tobacco shrub)*

Country code for walkers and motorists

Experienced ramblers are used to following a 'country code', but tourists may unwittingly cause damage, harm animals, and even endanger their own lives. Please heed this country code.

- **Do not light fires**. Stub out cigarettes with care.
- **Do not frighten animals**. By making loud noises or trying to touch or photograph them, you may cause them to run in fear and be hurt.
- **Walk quietly** through all hamlets and villages, and take care not to provoke any dogs. A walking stick is good protection against a menacing dog, but otherwise, keep it out of sight.
- **Leave all gates as you find them**. Although you may not see any animals, the gates *do* have a purpose.
- **Protect all wild and cultivated plants**. Don't try to pick wild flowers or uproot saplings. All fruit and other crops are someone's private property and should not be touched. *Never walk over cultivated land.*
- **Take all your litter away with you.**
- **Walkers — *do not take risks!*** Do not attempt walks beyond your capacity. **Never take a long hike on your own**, and *always* tell a responsible person exactly where you are going and what time you plan to return. Remember, if you become lost or injure yourself, it may be a long time before you are found. It's wise to carry some water, food and a cover-up.

● *Touring*

Paxos is not an ideal island for touring by car — there are no great sights or sites to see and, besides, it's only 9.5km long by 3km wide.

Cars can be rented through the tour companies or the agency in Gaios but, unless you consider a car essential for your holiday, I do advise against renting one. Touring can be done on **mopeds** or **motorbikes** and, yes, people of all ages get about this way on the island. Moreover, nearly all the scenic spots on the island are within a short stroll from the **bus** route.

If and when you hire a vehicle, there are important things to remember: always check it out before taking it on the road and report any dents and scratches, etc, lest you find that you get the blame for them. Have you got the necessaries: spare tyre, jack, enough petrol, the telephone numbers of the rental firm (both for office hours and after hours)? Do the lights work? *Read* the rental conditions and the insurance coverage documents.

Important: On Paxos some of the mopeds and bikes (or outboard motorboats, for that matter) **may not be insured**. You are liable for any damage you incur, and *it is always their estimate*. Be warned, too, that some of the mopeds and motorbikes may not be in good condition,

especially by the end of summer. Drive carefully, as there are a lot of novice riders on the roads, and in July and August getting around can be akin to a Shanghai rush hour.

One final word of caution: do note that there are only two **petrol stations** on the island, one just outside Gaios and the other at Magazia (both closed on Sundays and holidays).

Near Fontana/Platanos, sooty-faced and -socked sheep graze under the olive trees.

13

AROUND THE ISLAND

Gaios • Moggonissi Island • Gaios • Ozias • Gaios • Ag Apostoli Church• Fontana/Platanos • Loggos • Lakka • Ipapanti Church • Magazia • Fontana/ Platanos • Gaios

Distance: 35km/22mi; about 2-3 hours' driving

On route: Picnics 1-7 (see pages 8-11); Walks 1-7

The roads are generally narrow and twisting: sometimes we follow very small and rather bumpy lanes. Passing on these lanes is a problem. Drive slowly at all times, watching for livestock (and pedestrians near the villages). During high summer mopeds and motorbikes (and Italian tourists who have come by ferry in their own cars) jam the roads. Drive with care! There are only two petrol stations on the island, one just outside Gaios and the other in Magazia (closed Sundays and holidays).

Paxos is an island more suited to walking than to driving. I don't wish to discourage would-be motorists, but rather to encourage would-be walkers. Of course, if you have only a day or two, then you will want to see as much as possible. But here again, many of the beauty spots on Paxos are only accessible by foot or by sea. Perhaps that is why the island remains so special.

Under normal conditions, 35km could be covered in half an hour or so, but this is Paxos … where you will give the sheep and goats right of way on the tangle of lanes, stop to admire the beauty spots, and let time take care of itself.

Before heading to the north of the island from Gaios, I recommend two short 'side' excursions — to Moggonissi Island and Ozias.

To reach Moggonissi, squeeze past the waterfront houses at the southern end of Gaios and follow the coast. You pass the bronze statue of Georgis Anemoyiannis, a local hero who was burnt alive by the Turks during the 1821 Greek Revolution. He was captured after his failed attempt to set fire to the Turkish fleet. Your route runs close to the seashore for most of the way. Tiny secluded coves lie ensconced in the limestone-collared coastline. Olive groves cascade down the gentle inclines to the edge of the sea. Less than a kilometre out of town, you pass a taverna (✕) on the left and, shortly after, the rather discreet Paxos Beach Hotel (▲), sitting above a cove on a hillside, amidst olive trees.

Approaching **Moggonissi Island** (4km ✕) the olive groves subside and *maquis* takes over the country-

14

side; the greenery intensifies. The island sits across a shallow beryl-green inlet that narrows to a hair's breadth, only just making Moggonissi an island. Through this V one can see Antipaxos rising up out of the sea in the background. Moggonissi's small sandy beach and taverna (photograph pages 28-29) are very popular with those staying in Gaios, and taxi boats ply frequently between Gaios and the beach.

You *can* drive all the way to the beach and taverna

Gaios from the hills above the town. This photograph was taken not far from the track climbed at the start of Walk 3.

on a mostly concreted lane which crosses the causeway, then heads steeply uphill. But I recommend parking near the 6th-century church of Ag Marina (see photograph on page 9). Walk along the concrete lane, cross the causeway, then follow the shoreline along to the left. Walk 1 visits Moggonissi, and Picnic 1a is an especially pleasant setting for evening 'dining' in the open air.

Return to **Gaios**, then continue to Ozias: leave Gaios on the Makratika road (go left at the fork on the outskirts of town). Pass the petrol station (🚏) and climb into a small rocky valley stepped with olive groves. Barely a kilometre uphill you reach the Ozias turn-off, opposite the Paxos Club (⛰) and swimming pool. Turn left for Ozias. Colourful roadside gardens enliven the countryside here. Each garden has its complement of citrus, fig and pomegranate trees — and the enormous old ribbed water jars (see title page) which were once used for water storage, but are now only a decorative feature. Walls crippled by old age and derelict buildings sit back amidst the trees. The road meanders through this arcadian countryside, always in the shade of olive trees. In autumn the hillsides are flecked with carmine-coloured cyclamen, and you'll spy pockets of bright yellow *Sternbergia;* spring brings its own floral extravaganza, with deep blue bellflowers, lily-white arums, an assortment of anemones, and violet hyacinths.

Ozias (10km) is a pleasant country village straddling the top of a ridge. Small cottages line the side of

Ipapanti, the oldest church on Paxos (Walks 5 and 7; Picnic 7b). There's a photograph of the campanile on page 47.

Picnic 1b: the outlook over Mouzmouli Bay, a 20-30 minute walk from the church in Vellianitatika.

the road. This area was the first part of Paxos to be inhabited, and the settlement once spread as far as Vellianitatika. Descending back into **Gaios**, you may spot a mass of rubble from collapsed walls strewn about the slopes.

Now, to begin the 'real' tour, once again head up the Makratika road, soon passing the turn-off to Vellianitatika (Walk 2) on your left. If you were to park by the church in Vellianitatika, you could walk to two superb viewpoints: the outlook over Mouzmouli Bay shown here (Picnic 1b), and the equally fine overview of Galazio Bay shown on page 32 (Picnic 2a).

Just beyond the Vellianitatika turn-off, the 18th-century roadside church of Il Conde (also called Pantocratoras; ♔) in **Makratika** catches your attention with its fine campanile. The church door was made to order — the last Venetian mayor wanted to be able to enter the church on horseback! To enjoy Picnic 2b at Agrilas Beach, you would set off through the archway of the campanile.

The large, drawn-out village of **Bogdanatika** (13km ▲✕⊕; Walks 2 and 5) follows. Two more roads from Gaios join you from the right here. (Were you to fork off right along the New Port road, you could walk to the setting for Picnic 3 — the enchanting derelict hamlet of Geromonaches, shown on page 38.) As you leave Bogdanatika, you pass the turn-off left to Vlachopoulatika, a picturesque scattering of houses where you could potter around and stretch your legs, using the notes for Walk 5 on page 44.

Climbing the cypress-wooded slopes, you circle below the island's highest point — a hillock

231m/758ft high. The imposing 19th-century belfry of Ag Charalambos on the 'mountain' towers over the roadside. Rising high above the trees, it stands like a sentry post, looking out to the south of the island. You, too, look back to the south over undulating hills to Antipaxos and Lefkada beyond it.

Descending the 'mountainside', you enter **Magazia** (16km ✕🚍; Walk 5), soon turning left (just after a petrol station) on a tarmac lane signposted to Ag Apostoli. A kilometre down this narrow lane, turn up a track heading off right (between a garage and a house) onto the church driveway. **Ag Apostoli★** (17km 🛉🎗📷; Walk 5) is a very simple church, but you have really come for the view of the **Erimitis Cliffs★** — one of the 'sights' of Paxos. These glaring white limestone cliffs, shown on pages 22-23, plummet hundreds of feet into an aquamarine sea — a spell-binding sight. A table and benches here allow you to picnic in comfort (Picnic 5). Be sure, too, to stretch your legs by strolling from the church down to the superb viewpoint (📷) over Achai Bay and its cloistered caves, shown on page 45. Use the map or the notes on pages 45-46 to follow the coastal track to this nearby viewpoint. Ag Apostoli is kept locked, unfortunately, due to thievery in the past.

Back in **Magazia**, turn left and take the next right for Fontana/Platanos and Loggos. A flock of sooty-faced and -socked sheep graze amidst the trees (photograph pages 12-13). When you're out walking here, bells always alert you to their presence. **Fontana/Platanos**, half a kilometre further along, is where you turn left. The village boasts three *cafeneions* and as many churches. Walk 4 skirts the back of this village, and Walk 3 passes through it. Notice the olive press on the roadside, as you pass by the village (see drawing on page 2). Heaps of olive residue lie across the road from the press. You can't miss the resinous aroma. Paxos has only two modern olive presses, but there are still a number of the old ones about. In your strolls over the island you'll venture upon the remains of derelict presses. The process for making olive oil has remained unchanged. The olives are crushed with stone grinding wheels, and the pulp is then strained by pressing it through a layered sacking-like material, to rid it of lumps and foreign particles. At first the drained oil is dark and

*Old windmill
below Koutsi
(Short walk 3-3)*

cloudy, but eventually it clears. The final product is a very high-grade olive oil.

Winding down to Loggos, you pass the turn-off right to Kipos Beach (Picnic 4). On your left, you'll see a ruined windmill below, in a clearing amidst olive trees. Short walk 3-3 passes by this mill, shown above. Notice the extraordinary shape of the olive trees on these inclines. They have massive twisted and twirling trunks, and are pitted with 'eyes'. Nearer to the sea, colonnades of cypress trees line the roadside. Soon Levrechio Beach appears through the hillside trees. This white-stone cove is very popular, since it's the closest beach to Loggos.

Rounding a corner, you overlook a tight horseshoe-shaped bay and descend into **Loggos★** (22km ▲✕; Walks 3, 4, 6; Picnic 6). To me, this village, shown on pages 4-5 and 43, is the most appealing of the three fishing ports on Paxos. The pastel-coloured houses lean up against one another — as houses should in a real fishing village. And how's this for authenticity: you have to sidle past the houses and squeeze between the tables and chairs of the two waterfront restaurants to drive out of the village. Where else in the world would you drive straight through a restaurant? It's even more fun when you go through by bus — the diners quickly tuck in their toes! Loggos also seems to have more cats per capita than anywhere else in the world, so drive through with your foot on the brakes.

The enclosing hills make for good exploring. There are some derelict windmills (like the one shown above), tucked-away hamlets, beaches to suit all tastes, and most important of all, peace and quiet — outside July and August, that is. Climbing out of the deep valley that curves back inland behind Loggos, you meet a junction. Bear right for Lakka, your next port of call. Charming old villas grace the cool, shady olive groves.

Signs of mass tourism are non-existent on Paxos; however, coming into **Lakka**★ (25km ▲▲▲✗; Walks 5-7), one can't help but notice a couple of very ominous-looking apartment buildings. These days Lakka caters more for tourists than for fishermen. Two pincers of land embrace the shallow sandy-bottomed bay here, keeping it sheltered and calm — hence the deluge of sailboats and windsurfers. Somehow they even manage to water-ski amidst the confusion of craft. But if it's solitude you're after, you'll find it on Cape Lakka, where you can revel in superb landscapes and fine swimming spots. For children, the two beaches on the left side of the bay are ideal. Explore this headland using the notes for Picnic 7a (see photographs below and on pages 56-57).

On your return towards Gaios, take the wide road that disappears into a large valley burrowing into the hills behind Lakka. An unkempt forest of olive trees fills the valley floor. A kilometre along, turn off right on a concrete lane, to visit **Ipapanti Church**★ (☖) in **Grammatikeika**. Just over half a kilometre up this shady country lane, turn right on a narrower lane and then follows signs to the church. *Note:* The lane only

Lakka, from the promontory above the port. This is one of the delightful settings for Picnic 7a.

goes a couple of hundred metres towards the hamlet and then ends; *there is only parking space for a couple of cars.* You've come this far to see the church, not because it's an architectural masterpiece, but because it is the oldest on Paxos and atypical: two brothers built the church in 1601; the Ionian baroque bell-tower was added in 1772. And one cannot ignore its fine setting — high up on a densely wooded hillside deep in the tail of the valley, quite out of touch with the rest of Paxos. This is the setting for Picnic 7b; see photographs on pages 16 and 47.

Cercis siliquastrum
(Judas tree)

Heading home, return to the main road and bear right. At the Loggos/ Magazia junction keep right again. Ascending back over the island's backbone of hills, you look down into tree-clad valleys that wind their way seaward. You will have noticed that, on Paxos, the rural villages are made up of dispersed scatterings of houses, rather than forming a tight nucleus, as they do on Corfu, for example.

Sternbergia

Passing the Olive Press Museum, you are soon back in **Magazia** (32km). Turn left for **Fontana/ Platanos**, where you keep right. Pass through the village, keeping straight ahead, to take the coastal route back to Gaios. This road drops down to the coast, passing a reservoir in the valley on your right. You reach the sea at Kaki Lagada Beach (Walk 4) — an ideal spot to finish up the day with a refreshing dip. Winding around the eastern flanks, you pass above a couple more delectable coves, before joining the New Port road and descending back into **Gaios** (35km).

Acanthus spinosus

✿ Walking

Paxos is ideal for strolling, a place where you can amble along … oblivious of time and with no particular destination in mind. The countryside is gentle and friendly, the cove-indented coastline irresistible and fun to explore.

All the walks in this book are *graded* with the inexperienced walker in mind. Moreover, if you can't summon up the energy for several hours of rambling, have a look at the short walks described; they get you to all the island's beauty spots. Still too long a distance on foot? Then try the picnic suggestions — very short walks, especially suitable on really hot days.

Experienced ramblers will no doubt find all the walks in this book quite easy.

***Important*:** Times are given in the heading for each walk but, in summer particularly, a pleasant amble may — perhaps should — take twice as long. Take this into account when planning bus connections.

Where to stay

Paxos is so small that any part of the island can be reached within half an hour if you have a rented car or moped. The island is also relatively well served by bus and speedboat (to Moggonissi Island and Antipaxos).

The **three main tourist centres** are the ports of Gaios (the capital), Loggos and Lakka. In these places you can find villas, hotels, apartments or rooms. Remember that during the high season accommodation is *very* hard to find, if you have not booked it in advance.

Weather

The kindest months for your strolls around Paxos and Antipaxos are on either side of summer: April to June and September to October. July and August, when temperatures are mostly over 30°C, are the hot and sticky months — but sea breezes do help to keep you cool. This the time for short strolls only — to the beach or a picnic spot.

Spring is announced in April with warmth in the sun and an extravaganza of wild flowers, but the rain isn't over yet. By June a rainy day is considered unlucky, and in July or August, a phenomenon. Towards the end of September there's a freshness in the air again, with an occasional passing thunderstorm. In early October it's time for a cardigan and, as the month progresses, the cloudy days turn to rainy days. It's not the time for a beach holiday, but the haze-free cerulean sky and lush greenery, where autumn flowers hide, make this an exhilarating time to walk.

Nuisances

The chief problem one has to watch out for on Paxos is snakes. May and June is when the snakes come out to play ... and October, to a lesser extent. When walking in long grass, take a stick to beat the grass, and be vigilant around springs and water sources in the hot summer months. **Dogs** in general are no bother; they are

Picnic 5 affords this fabulous view over the Erimitis Cliffs

all bark and no bite. Threatening them with a stick or stone does the trick. **Scorpions** are nocturnal creatures, and the only time you'll encounter them is when you move logs or rocks. Do so carefully. Their sting is not dangerous, just very painful. **Bees** and **wasps** abound in summer, particularly around water. Approach all water sources and ponds, etc with care. If you are allergic to stings, make sure you have the necessary pills with you. Perhaps the biggest nuisance — but only in mid-summer — is the **horse-fly**. Long trousers and long-sleeved shirts lessen the problem. Avoid **ticks** by wearing long socks. Always watch out for **sea urchins** when swimming; they are found close to the shore in many coves and beaches. There is also a certain amount of illegal **bird-shooting**, but nothing like the slaughter of the past. If you hear shooting, make your presence known.

What to take

I've listed at the heading of each walk the minimum *year-round* equipment, relying on you to modify the list according to the season. Below is a check list of things to pack, if you plan to do a lot of walking.

walking boots or **sturdy shoes** (whichever you choose, they must be broken-in and comfortable)	**bandages and band-aids** plastic plates, cups etc.
waterproof rain gear (outside summer months)	**protective sun cream** **anorak** (zip opening) knives and openers
long trousers, tight at the ankles (sun and tick protection)	**sunhat, sunglasses** **antiseptic cream**
long-sleeved shirt (sun protection)	insect repellent
small rucksack	**cardigans**
extra pair of (long) socks	spare boot laces
plastic groundsheet	whistle
	torch

The items highlighted in bold type are mandatory. Please don't ruin your holiday with a sprained ankle or sunstroke. Always carry a sunhat, long-sleeved shirt and long trousers with you, and put them on when you have had enough sun. Take your lunch in a shady spot on hot days, and carry a good supply of fruit and water.

Greek for walkers

In the majority of the tourist areas you hardly need to know any Greek, but once you are out in the countryside a few words of the language will be helpful. Anyway, it is nice to be able to communicate, if only a little, and people warm to your attempts.

Here's one way to ask directions in Greek and understand the answers you get! First memorise the few 'key' and 'secondary' questions given below. Then, *always follow up your key question with a second question demanding a yes (ne) or no (ochi) answer.* Greeks invariably raise their heads to say 'no', which looks to us like the beginning of a 'yes'! (By the way, 'ochi'(no) might be pronounced as **o**-hee, **o**-shee or even **oi**-ee.)

Following are the two most likely situations in which you may need to use some Greek. The dots (...) show where you will fill in the name of your destination. Ask someone who lives on the island to help you with the pronunciation of place names.

■ *Asking the way*

The key questions

English	Approximate Greek pronunciation
Good day, greetings	**Hair**-i-tay
Hello, hi (informal)	**Yas**-sas(plural); **Yia**-soo(singular)
Please —	**Sas** paraka**loh** —
Where is	**Pou ee**-nay
the road to...?	o **thro**-mo stoh...?
the footpath to...?	ee mono-**pati** stoh...?
the bus stop?	ee **sta**ssis?
Many thanks.	Eff-hah-ree-**stoh** po-li.

Secondary question leading to a yes/no answer

English	Approximate Greek pronunciation
Is it here?	**Ee**-nay e**tho**?
Is it there?	**Ee**-nay eh-**kee**?
Is it straight ahead?	**Ee**-nay kat-eff-**thia**?
Is it behind?	**Ee**-nay **pee**-so?
Is it to the right?	**Ee**-nay thex-**ya**?
Is it to the left?	**Ee**-nay aris-teh-**rah**?
Is it above?	**Ee**-nay eh-**pano**?
Is it below?	**Ee**-nay **kah**-to?

■ *Asking a taxi driver to take you somewhere and return for you, or asking a taxi driver to collect you*

English	Approximate Greek pronunciation
Please —	**Sas** paraka**loh** —
Would you take us to ...?	Tha **pah**-reh mas stoh...?
Come and pick us up from ... at ...	**El**-la na mas **pah**-reh-teh apo ... stees ...

(Instead of memorising the hours of the day simply point out on your watch the time you wish to be collected.)

1 GAIOS • VELLIANITATIKA • MOUZMOULI CLIFFS • TRIPITOS ARCH • OZIAS • MOGGONISSI ISLAND • GAIOS

See also photographs pages 9, 17, cover

Distance: 9km/5.5mi; 3h50min

Grade: fairly easy, if you exclude the descent to the Tripitos Arch. If you do the whole walk, the grade is moderate to strenuous. The descent to the Tripitos Arch follows a goats' path, with the **possibility of vertigo** — *only recommended in dry weather.*

Equipment: sturdy shoes or walking boots, sunhat, suncream, long-sleeved shirt, long trousers, cardigan, rainwear, bathing suit, picnic, water

How to get there: 🚌 to Gaios or the Vellianitatika turn-off
To return: 🚌 from Gaios

Short walks

1 Gaios — Vellianitatika — Mouzmouli cliffs — Gaios: 2h; easy; access/return as above. Follow the entire walk, but exclude the descent to the Tripitos Arch and the Moggonissi section.

2 Gaios — Vellianitatika — Tripitos Arch — Gaios: 2h30min; moderate to strenuous; access/return as above. Follow the main walk to the Tripitos Arch. Once back on the main path, turn off left after a few metres (yards), to make for Ozias, from where you can follow the road back to Gaios. (See notes page 30.)

Tripitos Arch is one of the island's natural wonders. It takes you by surprise: you peer over the sheer sea-cliffs and see not far below you an impressive archway of rock hanging off the island. It requires a bit of a scramble to reach the arch but, if you're sure-footed, don't miss this descent. Otherwise, just enjoy the peace and quiet of the shady mule tracks we follow. Then cross the short causeway to Moggonissi Island and take a dip in the beautiful inlet that lights up this picturesque corner of Paxos.

Start the walk from the main square *(platia)* in **Gaios**: leave on the road that climbs to Makratika. When it forks, a minute out, keep left. This country road ascends steadily into the spine of modest hills that runs down the centre of the island. Twisted old olive trees lean out over the road. Paxos seems to be one extended canopy of olive groves — they cover most of the island and have done so since the Venetian era. It's estimated that the island supports some 300,000 of them. It is said that a well-nurtured tree is able to produce up to 20 kilos of olive oil in a good year.

Crumbled stone walls terrace the rocky limestone hillsides. Around **10min** uphill, opposite the PAXOS CLUB, you pass the OZIAS TURN-OFF. Barely a minute

26

beyond it, reach a bar/restaurant on the left, off a curve. Leave the road here and take the path round the back of the restaurant (walking through the dining area), soon passing a CHURCH on your left. Just before you reach the Ozias road on the left, keep along a path above the road, on the right, and then turn right uphill on a mule track. This wide cobbled trail climbs to Vellianitatika; a high stone wall lines the right-hand side of the trail, and terracing litters the slope.

Tripitos Arch

At the junction below the *platia* in **Vellianitatika** keep straight ahead (the left-hand path will be your ongoing route, when you return from the viewpoint ahead). Go past a SHRINE and the CAMPANILE of the church. Beyond is the church itself, which backs onto the *platia*. Some 30m/yds beyond the campanile, opposite the CHURCH, turn left up a stepped alley between walls. On meeting a crossing footpath, turn left and, after passing an isolated cottage, descend between crumbling walls. The path narrows, then suddenly you emerge on the cliffs to the north of Mouzmouli Bay. In spring and early summer this open coastal *maquis* is brilliant with the fierce yellows of broom, gorse and Jerusalem sage.

Return to the junction below the village *platia*, and now turn right. Once through the houses, curve left on an earthen path. Circling a solitary house with a garden on your left, you come to a junction and turn right along a driveway. Then branch off the drive onto the first path heading off to the right. Stone walls hem you in. When the next junction (which looks more like a square) brings you to a halt, head to the right, towards the coast. Ignore the narrow alleys leading off the path.

Some 15 minutes from Vellianitatika you're at the very edge of the cliffs rising to the south of **Mouzmouli Bay**. This gaping bite out of the coastline, shown on page 17, is the setting for Picnic 1b. **Cape Chiros** lies below. Approach the cliffs with care, especially if you are picnicking — it's a fairly precarious perch so near to the cliff-edge. A footpath leads off towards the headland, but after 10 minutes it peters out in a mass of boulders and old terraces. It is better to leave the cape to the seagulls and reserve your energy for the Tripitos Arch.

To continue the walk, return to the square-like junction, three minutes back from the picnic

The sandy beach on Moggonissi Island is very popular (and safe for young children); a taverna hides in the trees.

spot, and this time head along the alley to the right. Leave it alongside an OLIVE PRESS, to take a concrete lane which ends metres/yards further uphill. A garden flooded with colour sits at the end of the lane. Follow the paved path that heads along the right-hand side of the garden. But before you reach the adjacent house, turn right up steps (do not continue straight ahead). Follow the main path, and you pass through a friendly cluster of houses buried amidst the olive groves high on the hillside. Tired stone walls age the face of the countryside like wrinkles.

Minutes along, you descend onto a wider track and keep right. A minute uphill there is a three-way junction, where a blue door in the wall is a useful landmark. (*Note:* Two minutes up the alley on your immediate right lies one of the best-preserved windmills on the island. Inside it are the remains of a staircase. *With care* one can clamber up these stairs for an excellent panorama over the centre of the island — worth a detour!)

Your ongoing route to Tripitos lies along the major track to the left. The broad track soon swings right towards the coast and the arch. Just after passing a green metal gate on your right, a faded sign points the way to 'TRIPITOS', down a footpath on the right-hand side of the track. Follow this path downhill. In autumn pink-flowering heather brightens up the countryside on this descent. Edging around the inner slopes of a small, narrow valley, you come to the plummeting coastline. More dramatic seascapes unravel; the island topples off into the sea.

Descending further, bear right and step over a flattened bit of fence. A goats' path takes you down the steep hillside. *Go carefully; the cliff-edge is very close by on the left!* Shortly (**1h30min**), **Tripitos Arch** is in sight: a towering limestone rock joined to the island by a thin arch. At least it looks very narrow, until you are actually crossing it. The descent is more awkward than vertiginous and soon you're high above the sea, crossing the arch. (But *don't* attempt this crossing on windy days!)

Returning from Tripitos, follow the track back the way you came. After six minutes, where the track swings left, turn right along a narrow path between stone walls. *(Note: If you are doing Short walk 2, or if you wish to get back to civilisation and a bar as soon as possible, take the turn-off to the left after a few metres/yards.)* After two minutes, the path passes a roofless building on the right. Continue along the path for another two minutes, to meet a wide, stony track running between walls. Turn left along this track and, after cresting a small rise (with a house, perhaps still under construction, on the right), continue downhill into the olive trees. Keeping down this partly concreted track, you reach a tarmac road in six minutes. Follow this to the right to reach **Ozias** (**2h10min**), where you can have a drink at the small bar/shop opposite the church before deciding whether to press on to Moggonissi.

To make for Moggonissi from Ozias, descend the concrete track opposite the corner of the CHURCH (where the road bends round the building). At the bottom of the dip there is a WELL. Beyond it rise the hills overlooking Moggonissi Island. Keep straight ahead at a crossing lane/track (leading to Yftika and Agoratika) and continue along a wide, dusty track through attractive open countryside.

After 10 minutes or so, Moggonissi — a low mound of trees and *maquis* — comes into view, and the track (now with a concrete surface) descends towards the coast. A shallow turquoise-green inlet separates the island from Paxos. Reaching the shore-

A typical stone-laid mule track

line, turn right along the road, soon arriving at a small beach with the remains of the early Christian basilica of **Ag Marina** behind it. Walking along the water's edge, you look down into the limpid green sea. When the sealed road ends, follow the concrete lane leading off it (this lane leads to Picnic 1a; see photograph on page 9). You circle the base of a hillock which is thickly wooded in cypress trees. Minutes on, a causeway takes you across the inlet, which is narrow at this point.*

Once over the causeway and on **Moggonissi Island** (**3h**), follow the rocky shoreline path to the left, to reach the taverna and a beach of imported sand. To the right, both sides of the inlet offer good views of the cliff-bashing sea and Antipaxos. On the north side of the inlet, you can scale up the sea-cliffs to your right, to see the striking limestone rock formations. The precipitous and curving coastline resembles a succession of ancient Roman amphitheatres: a particularly fine spot to wind up the walk.

Return to Gaios along the coast road. Although tarmac all the way, it does not carry much traffic and provides pretty views along the shoreline. Soon after passing the PAXOS BEACH HOTEL, you can take a short-cut round the back of the beach. Give yourself 50 minutes or so to reach **Gaios** (**3h50min**). Or, if your legs won't carry you any further, there is a late afternoon taxi boat from the beach at Moggonissi back to Gaios, but only when the taverna is open.

Note: Intrepid walkers might like to venture over to Kaltonissi Island to see the wild setting of the Ag Spiridon Chapel. Once over the causeway, keep right and remain close to the coast. Allow 20-30 minutes and expect scratched legs, twisted ankles, and a ruined pair of shoes ... but expect to enjoy yourself as well! A short swim across the channel that separates the islands will get you to the church. Watch out for the giant-sized billy-goat that rules Kaltonissi ... and good luck!

Distance: 7km/4.3mi; 2h30min

Grade: easy to moderate. Gentle descents and ascents, sometimes on rocky paths. *Not recommended in wet weather.*

Equipment: sturdy shoes, sunhat, suncream, long-sleeved shirt, long trousers, cardigan, rainwear, bathing suit, picnic, water

How to get there: 🚌 to Gaios or to the Vellianitatika turn-off
To return: 🚌 from Gaios

Short walks (even shorter if you start at the Vellianitatika turn-off)

1 Gaios — Vellianitatika — Galazio Bay — Vellianitatika — Gaios: 1h30min; easy; access/return as above. Follow the main walk to the Galazio Bay overlook and retrace your steps.

2 Gaios — Makratika — Agrilas Beach — Makratika — Gaios: 2h; quite easy; access/return as above. Use the map to reach Makratika by road and then refer to the last three lines on page 33 ('… in Makratika… Head through the archway …'). Follow the walk to the end.

H ere's a splendid walk to whet your appetite — an apéritif. Crossing the island (which is only 3km across at its widest point) from east to west, you sample the rural charm of Paxos. Then, once out of the cloak of olive groves, superb sea views greet you.

Start out in **Gaios** by using the notes for WALK 1, to reach the bar/restaurant just above the OZIAS TURN-OFF. Pass the bar, and after 30m/yds turn left, to ascend a concrete path between walls to Vellianitatika. (*Note:* This is *not* the path just behind the restaurant, which is followed in Walk 1.) About two minutes uphill, pass through a junction (bearing right) and join a driveway which emerges on a tarmac road alongside the CHURCH in **Vellianitatika (15min)**. Continue past the church. Derelict buildings, and houses partially obscured in plant-crammed gardens, sit

Picnic 2a: This wonderful outlook over Galazio Bay is reached 20-25 minutes from Vellianitatika. Unfortunately, this splendid beach is only accessible by boat. But Agrilas Beach, the inlet on the other side of the slender spit of land north of Galazio, can be reached on foot (Picnic 2b).

back in the trees. Notice how tall these olive trees are. Some attain a height of 15m/50ft and can live for up to 1500 years!

After four minutes, where the tarmac ends, follow the concrete track swinging right between stone walls. Cypresses pierce the silvery-green mantle of the olive trees. Pass by the small church of **Ag Dimitrios**, on the right, and continue along the track, ignoring a turn-off to the right. Four minutes past Ag Dimitrios you pass a large, isolated house on the right. The track now becomes rougher and ends two minutes later, at a set of METAL GATES in a wall. Walk between two olive trees and bear left along a stony path between walls. Clumps of red-berried *Pistacia lentiscus* now become noticeable. The resin from this shrub is supposed to preserve the gums — and cure toothache as well. Garden plots hide behind the walls. A lean grove of cypress trees provides a brief interlude before you emerge into the *maquis* — an impenetrable blanket of low bushy (and often thorny) scrub. On Paxos this consists chiefly of spiny broom *(Calicotome villosa)*, Spanish broom *(Spartium junceum)*, *Pistacia lentiscus,* myrtle, Mediterranean buckthorn, and kermes oak.

A minute out of the trees the stupendous cliff-top view over **Galazio Bay** shown opposite awaits you (**40min**; Picnic 2a). Not too close to the edge! You look across a succession of sweeping bays bound by towering cliffs. Valleys slice back off them, leaving narrow inlets in their wake. Far below you lies a white stony beach that dips into a pale blue sea. Unfortunately, this enticing beach is only accessible by boat. The path quickly fades as it descends along the edge of the cliff. Go with care. Low bushy juniper shrubs dot the sea-slope and, with luck, you may spot a few swallow-tail butterflies.

When you're ready to leave this exhilarating spot, return to **Vellianitatika** (**1h**) and follow the road back towards Gaios. Two minutes beyond Vellianitatika, on the outside of the first hairpin bend, turn left into an alley descending through houses. You emerge on the main road just below your next turn-off, by the charming little Venetian church of **Il Conde** (also called 'Pantocratoras') in **Makratika**. *(Short walk 2 joins here.)* Head through the archway of the impressive campanile. The last of the Venetian mayors had

On our way to Agrilas beach, we come upon some curious stone buildings below Makratika.

a doorway specially built to enable him to enter the church on his horse.

Beyond the church ignore the wide crossing track leading to the houses on your left; keep straight on along the right-hand side of the valley. Descending amidst a mass of stone wall terracing, you come upon the curious buildings shown above: one resembles a shrine, the other is conical. Beyond and below these two sits another which houses a well with a large trough outside, hewn from the solid rock. Skirt to the left of this building, and follow the remains of a faint, overgrown goats' trail. Descending gently down the valley, bear left after 200m/yds, down through olive trees and then a belt of thick vegetation. You reach a stony vehicle track. The bracken of the upper valley gives way to heather, kermes oak, *Pistacia lentiscus,* and *Coronilla emerus* (Scorpian senna, which has clusters of brilliant yellow flowers in spring).

Turn right and follow the track downhill; there is a short scramble at the end of the track, which drops you onto **Agrilas Beach** (**1h30min**; Picnic 2b). This secluded stony cove is one of the few accessible swimming places on the west coast of the island. Look out for spiny sea-urchins if swimming off the rocks! The bladed crest of the rocky promontory on your left (the spit of land you can see in the photograph on page 32) offers you another fine view to Galazio Bay. *Limonium bellifolium, Crithmum maritimum* (rock samphire, a fleshy, pale yellow-flowering plant, sometimes collected for pickling), and *Anthyllis hermanniae* (a small spiny shrub that has bright yellow flowers in spring) sprout between the rocks.

Refreshed and homeward bound, return the same way to **Makratika** (**2h**). Back at the church of Il Conde (Pantocratoras), follow the main road uphill to the left. Ten minutes up, at the Gaios junction in **Bogdanatika** (**2h10min**), turn right and descend to **Gaios** (**2h 30min**).

3 GAIOS • GEROMONACHES • FONTANA/ PLATANOS • KANGATIKA • LOGGOS

See also photographs on pages 10, 12-13, 15, 19, 43

Distance: 5.5km/3.5mi; 2h15min

Grade: fairly strenuous ascent at the start of the walk; otherwise easy. The beginning of the walk is *not recommended in wet weather* (when you could substitute Short walk 2 below).

Equipment: sturdy shoes, sunhat, suncream, long-sleeved shirt, long trousers, cardigan, rainwear, bathing suit, picnic, water

How to get there: 🚐 to Gaios
To return: 🚐 from Loggos

Short walks

1 Gaios — Geromonaches — Fontana/Platanos: 1h10min; grade, access as above; return by 🚐 from Fontana/Platanos. Follow the main walk to Fontana/Platanos.

2 Fontana/Platanos — Kangatika — Loggos: 45min; easy; 🚐 to Fontana/Platanos and return from Loggos. Pick up the main walk at the 1h10min-point and follow it to the end.

3 Loggos — Koutsi — Marmari Beach — Loggos: 1h10min; moderate to strenuous, with a very steep initial ascent and some scrambling on the paths between the beaches; 🚐 to and from Loggos. Take the Lakka road out of Loggos and climb the first steep lane cutting off to the left. Keep right all the way up and, in five minutes, reach a tightly bunched hamlet. Ascend the steps and pass through the houses, bearing neither right nor left. Meet a track on the far side of the hamlet and follow it. In a minute you head through a confusion of tracks at an intersection: keep to the main, middle, track. Approaching the trunk of the derelict windmill shown on page 19, come to a fork. Take the branch to the left, which takes you through Koutsi and out onto the main road. Turn right and, a minute uphill, turn off left down a tarmac road. Three minutes along keep straight on through a junction, cross a crest, and descend past Villa Chrissa. From here you have a choice of routes back to Loggos, and you can explore the pretty coastline and its many coves. (See map and notes for Walk 4, page 42, second paragraph.)

Climbing into the hills that look out over the harbour at Gaios, we stumble upon the abandoned and enchanting hamlet of Geromonaches. Sitting here amidst the sagging walls and derelict buildings, time really does stand still. Continuing on, we traipse over the island's backbone of hills. Rustic villages dot the countryside; these too echo abandonment, with their shuttered villas and forgotten gardens ... idyllic spots for day-dreaming.

Start the walk where the bus turns round in **Gaios**. Take a side-road towards the **Church of the Apostles** — easy to spot because of its leaning campanile! Pass the church and turn left. Ahead you will see the wide steps of the neglected-looking *sterna* (town water tank). At the bottom of the steps, take the path to the left and then climb a short flight of steps. Joining the town BYPASS ROAD to the New Port, bear right.

From a bend, some three minutes along, you have a tremendous view over this very photogenic fishing port (see page 15) and the pine studded island of St Nicholas. Leave the road here, just as it curves round to the left: head left up a steep concrete path. After passing two houses on your left, take a small goats' trail climbing the hillside on the left. The tall stems of autumn-flowering sea-squill fleck the terraced inclines. Ignore side paths; keep right and uphill. As you climb, the bay unravels into a stunning sight, with its blends of greens and blues from the vegetation and the sea. Boats dot the inlet, which looks more like a river where it curls around St Nicholas. You spot, too, some remnants of the islet's Venetian fortress (1423), its ramparts swallowed up amidst a tangle of shrubs and trees.

The smaller island beyond St Nicholas is Panayia. It is home to a nunnery and the 17th-century church of Moni Panagias, built on the site of an earlier place of Christian worship and said to contain the finest decorations of any church on Paxos. There is a procession to the church each year on 14th August, the saint's day.

Spent shotgun cartridges littering the ground testify to the wealth of birds in this area. Soon a valley slides away below you and you reach a concrete lane (**25min**). Turn left uphill, then, almost immediately, turn right on a good track through olive groves. A couple of minutes along, the track ends. Paths fork off both left and right. A SHRINE (which looks rather like a public WC) stands inside the left-hand fork. Geromonaches is still in hiding at this point. Head up to the left, and the hamlet soon discloses itself. You can peer into the doorways of the derelict buildings which line the crumbling walls beside the mule track. Some houses have been restored in recent years, as this formerly abandoned village reawakens. **Geromonaches** (**30min**; Picnic 3; see photograph on the next page) is one of my favourite spots on Paxos, and I hope you enjoy it as much as I do.

When the path forks at a HOUSE WITH A RED DOOR, bear left uphill. The path becomes overgrown, but it runs along the line of a wall, past two derelict buildings on the right. Further up the path, swing to the right between stone walls. Turn left at the high stone wall ahead, to rejoin the main track and there go right. (*Note:* If you turn *left* on the main track you will quickly regain your outgoing route, from where you can retrace your steps to Gaios.)

On the top of the crest, small outcrops of limestone are a dominant feature of the landscape. You have a view across the eastern flank of Paxos to the tail of Corfu, and over to Epirus. Five minutes after joining the track, the surface becomes concrete and passes two houses on the right. Then the concrete swings right, to meet the road (**50min**), where you turn left. In two minutes meet a junction in **Bogdanatika**. Head right along the LOGGOS ROAD. The prominent campanile of **Agios Charalambos**, thrusting up through cypress trees on the hillside ahead, serves as a landmark in the surrounding countryside.

A minute above the Vlachopoulatika junction, at a sharp uphill bend, fork right on a broad track to the left of a house. The inclines are cloaked in a thicket of greenery, with trees and bushes vying for space. Five minutes along, as the broad track

Bright pink belladonna lilies light up the shadows of the olive groves, not far outside Fontana/Platanos. On Paxos and Corfu the olives are left to fall from the trees. You'll often see netting overhead, above the mule tracks. It's tied between the trees to catch the olives as they fall. In the Mediterranean and the rest of Greece, the trees are generally beaten to make the olives fall.

begins to turn the flank of the hill, it ends abruptly at a GATEWAY. At this point take a goats' trail leading uphill to the left. Be careful along this stretch; it's a menace of jutting lumps of rock. Ignore paths descending to the right. Keep close to the wall on the left and continue uphill. You clamber through a narrow section of path, hemmed in by large stones, and come to a fork with a pine tree in the middle. There is a very large olive tree standing behind it on the left: bear left here (there *may* be a small stone cairn marker). Fork right on a faint track for a few paces, and cross some bedrock, to join the fairly decent track below you on the right. You are now on the way to Fontana/Platanos. (*Note:* If you are doing this walk in reverse, this obscure turn-off lies 100 paces below the village parking area and 17 paces before a stone wall below the track on your left.)

The track becomes a concreted road and you enter **Fontana/Platanos** (**1h10min**). (*Short walk 1 ends here and Short walk 2 begins here.*) Turn left when you reach the tarmac road and walk through the village, with its large CHURCH AND CAMPANILE on the left. The church is set back from the road, with a large plane tree *(platanos)* in front, making an attractive square. The original, Italian, name for the village (Fontana) has been replaced by the Greek word, Platanos; both names now appear on signs. Once through the village, follow the right-hand road towards LOGGOS (left goes to Magazia).

Continue along the road *(passing the turning where Walk 4 joins from the right)*, then pass a blue and white SHRINE on the left and, a little later, VILLA ANTHEA, also on the left. About 10 minutes from Fontana/Platanos, fork left on a concrete lane

Spare the time for delightful old abandoned hamlets like Geromonaches, shown here — one of my favourite spots on Paxos (Picnic 3).

signposted to **Zernatika**. Follow this gently uphill and continue past a clump of houses. By OLIVE TREE HOUSE the concrete underfoot gives way to stone. At the next track junction, look out for a STONE COTTAGE WITH A BLUE FENCE on the left. Pass this and keep straight on; the way ends outside a cottage with a GREEN GARDEN GATE. Here steps take you down to a tarmac road just below. Bear left here and pass through **Kangatika** — a sprinkling of houses and, further on, a CHURCH. This area makes for some superb rambling. Continue past VILLA LAVANDA on the right.

Cyclamen

The remains of a windmill can be seen through the trees, crowning the top of a crest below. *(Short walk 3 would take you past this windmill; see photograph page 19.)* Windmills — used for the grinding of corn, maize and barley — were once a noticeable feature of the island's landscape; there were some 16 of them. Now, unfortunately, only the shells of these mills remain, thanks to the vandalism of the occupying forces during World War II. Walk 1 passes close to one of the best-preserved windmills on Paxos.

Euphorbia dendroides (Tree spurge)

Vitex agnus-castus (Chaste tree)

Dropping down the flank of a valley through olive trees, the lane (now concrete) grows steeper — put on the brakes! It twists and winds all the way down to the valley floor, where you meet the LAKKA/LOGGOS ROAD. Turn right into **Loggos (2h15min)**. Time for a cool beer, and there is no better place to have it than looking out over this exquisite little bay, shown on pages 4-5 and 43.

Senecio

Juniperus oxycedrus (Juniper)

4 GAIOS • KAKI LAGADA BEACH • FONTANA/PLATANOS • KIPIADI BEACH • LOGGOS

See also photograph pages 4-5

Distance: 6km/3.7mi; 2h50min

Grade: moderate to strenuous for less experienced walkers, quite easy for fit ramblers. A short but steep ascent midway. *Not recommended in wet weather.*

Equipment: sturdy shoes, sunhat, suncream, long-sleeved shirt, long trousers, cardigan, rainwear, bathing suit, picnic, water

How to get there: 🚌 to Gaios
To return: 🚌 from Loggos

Short walks

1 **Gaios — Kaki Lagada Beach — Fontana/Platanos:** 50min; grade and access as above. A lovely beach and an uphill scramble. Follow the main walk to Fontana/Platanos, then return by 🚌.

2 **Loggos — Levrechio Beach — Marmari Beach — Kipos Beach:** 30min return; easy, but along roughish paths; 🚌 to and from Loggos. Use the map to reach these beaches; the route is straightforward.

This hike takes you to the picturesque fishing village of Loggos, shown on pages 4-5 and 43. Along the walk you dip down into enticing little coves, sampling them as you go, and climb out again, weaving your way through thickets of cypress trees.

To start the walk, leave **Gaios** along the HARBOUR-SIDE ROAD to the New Port, with moored boats and yachts lining the route. Where the road swings inland towards Platanos, Magazia and Loggos (**25min**), take the wide descending road turning off right. A tangle of scrub and trees covers the sea-slopes. Epirus lies over to your right, and up ahead the bright limestone cliffs of Cape Asprokavos (the setting for Walk 20 in *Landscapes of Corfu*) glare across at you. Reaching the coast in five minutes, you pass little **Kioni Gouli Beach**, overlooked by the Anessa Apartments. Next you pass **Kamini Beach**, shingly and clean, with a small parking area behind it. Then, 15 minutes after the turning, **Kaki Lagada Beach** (**40min**) comes into view. Reach it by a wooden staircase or continue along the road and follow a track down to the beach, where there are stone tables with seats and plenty of shade.

Kipiadi Beach seen through cypress trees. This bright-white beach lights up the entire landscape.

40

Villa Delphini sits above the northern end of this quiet beach, which everyone seems to ignore.

To continue the walk, go up the remains of a concrete ramp leading to Villa Delphini and turn left up a steep, rocky and overgrown path, keeping close to the garden wall. You'll need your long sleeves and trousers here. There is another wall, topped with concrete posts, on your left. After several minutes' scramble, you emerge on the villa's concrete drive, with its gated entrance beside you. Follow the drive uphill. From now on you can enjoy the superb view of the west coast and the mainland.

A steep climb now takes you up through tall dark green spires of cypress. Turn left at the T-junction five minutes uphill. Entering cool olive groves, the way eases out. Ignore the track joining from the left. About 15 minutes from Villa Delphini, on the outskirts of **Fontana/Platanos** (**1h**), leave the concrete road and turn right on a farm track. Ahead of you there is a large stone house on the left, with terracotta pots sitting on the boundary wall. In five minutes you pass an inland boatyard on the left and reach a tarmac lane (where a small CHURCH stands 100m/yds along another lane to your right). Continue straight ahead along this lane, to join the main Fontana/Platanos– Loggos road after five minutes. Turn right along this smooth stretch of tarmac, where there is little traffic. *(Or turn left to end Short walk 1 with a cooling drink in one of the bars).*

Heading towards Loggos, you soon pass a blue and

white SHRINE on the left. Then walk past Villa Anthea (also on the left). About 10 minutes along the road you pass a concrete lane on the left, signposted to ZERNATIKA.* Then, about a mile from Fontana/ Platanos, the road turns sharply downhill to the right, with a side-road on the left leading to KANGATIKA. *Attention!* Just 20m/yds below this bend you can take an interesting short-cut. Step over a WATER PIPE on the right and you will find a narrow, almost-hidden path. This drops down from the main road to join an old BRITISH MILITARY ROAD, with finely engineered stone retaining walls. After a couple of zigzags, rejoin the main road and follow it downhill until it swings hard left. At this bend there are several villa signs, a tarmac road, and two concrete lanes on the right. Turn right along the tarmac road, passing the village *sterna* (water tank) behind a wall on the left, with a chapel beyond it. Just past a house on the right, at a crossroads, turn right for KIPIADI BEACH. Follow the concrete lane downhill, ignoring side-turnings. When the concrete ends, continue down for 100m/yds, then turn sharp right on a stony track through olive and cypress trees to the coastal *maquis* behind Kipiadi. Five minutes along, turn left on a narrow path at the corner of a wall. **Kipiadi Beach (1h50min)** itself is rather a disappointment (unless a storm chances to clean it up), but there are plenty of beautiful coves ahead.

Return uphill to the crossroads and turn right, now heading towards Loggos. After a pleasant easy stroll you pass VILLA CHRISSA. About 60m/yds beyond Villa Chrissa, directly opposite a house (under construction at time of writing), descend a path on the left.** You soon pass through a cool thicket of trees. Drop down some steps, ignore turnings to the right, and continue downhill to the left as the path rounds the shoulder of the hill. At the bottom you reach the tiny hamlet of

*You could take a short, extremely pleasant detour here, following the route of Walk 3 through Zernatika and Kangatika. Ascend this lane and pick up the notes for Walk 3 at the top of page 39. Follow this diversion to the cottage with steps leading down to the road and then turn right, back to the Loggos road.

Or first make another detour — to Kipos Beach, another tourist-brochure cove: continue down the concrete lane and, when you reach a garden wall ahead, bear right alongside it, following a stony track to VILLA PANORAMA. The track ends here, but a path drops steeply down to **Kipos Beach, setting for Picnic 4, less than 10 minutes from Villa Chrissa.)

Marmari. With the entrance to MARMARI STONE HOUSE on your left, turn right along another stony path beside a garden wall. In two minutes you're at **Marmari Beach** — secluded, quiet, and shady. From here return to Marmari Stone House and turn right along a track, to reach **Levrechio Beach** in a minute. This cove is more popular than the others along the walk ... because Loggos is just around the corner. A few modest villas overlook this stony beach.

To make for Loggos, take the concrete lane out and turn right when you meet the road. Stone steps on the right lead down to a rocky bathing platform at the water's edge. A couple of minutes down you're in the friendly seaside village of **Loggos (2h50min)**. Bar ΕΥΡΩΠΗ is the perfect place to put your feet up — you won't find a friendlier bar anywhere.

Accommodation on Paxos is chiefly in villas. Some are extremely luxurious and in secluded surroundings; others, like bright-white 'Marika' here at the port in Loggos afford a taste of Greek life right in the heart of a small community. (Taken from Bar ΕΥΡΩΠΗ.)

5 BOGDANATIKA • VLACHOPOULATIKA • AG APOSTOLI CHURCH • MAGAZIA • IPAPANTI CHURCH • LAKKA

See also photographs pages 16, 20, 22-23

Distance: 9.5km/6mi; 2h30min. (If walking from Gaios, add 20min to all timings.)

Grade: fairly easy, but quite long.

Equipment: sturdy shoes (or walking boots, if you're doing the detour to Erimitis Bay), sunhat, suncream, long-sleeved shirt, long trousers, cardigan, rainwear, bathing suit, picnic, water

How to get there: 🚐 to Bogdanatika
To return: 🚐 from Lakka

Short walks

1   **Bogdanatika — Vlachopoulatika — Ag Apostoli — Magazia:** 1h15min; fairly easy; access as above. Follow the main walk to Magazia, from where you can return by 🚐.

2   **Magazia — Ipapanti — Lakka:** 1h15min; easy; 🚐 to Magazia. Follow the main walk from the 1h15min-point and return by 🚐 from Lakka.

H ere's a walk *without beaches!* It's a real country-side ramble — most of it spent wandering through rustic villages deep amidst the olive groves. But a walk without sea views would be virtually impossible on this tiny island, and this walk has per-haps the most dramatic sea views you'll see on Paxos.

Get off the bus in **Bogdanatika**, at the VLACHO-POULATIKA JUNCTION. You'll spot a bar beside the road, on your left. **Set off** by taking the concrete lane leading off to the right of the bar, with a SPORTS GROUND on the right. In one minute, at a lane junction, bear right; after 50m/yds, the lane turns sharp right uphill. It soon reverts to a stony surface and narrows to a path between walls. Follow the path past a stone wall with copings on the right and another walled path on the left. Passing close to some scattered dwellings, the path continues its winding course between walls and then joins a wider track on an outside bend. The modern central SCHOOL is off to the right. Turn left along the track and, a minute later, where the track bears off left, go straight ahead on a walled path. In another minute you reach the con-crete drive to a house, with its entrance gates beside you on the left. Now turn right and, in 100m/yds come to a tarmac road. Turn left and, in a minute, turn left at a junction, to explore the pretty village of **Vlachopoulatika** (**12min**). The heart of the village is a short distance ahead.

Then return to the road junction and turn left

44

downhill. This wider road soon leads you gently uphill through pine and cypress woods and olive groves, with views down to the coast. Some 15 minutes after leaving Vlachopoulatika, at the top of the incline, another tarmac road joins from the right. In three minutes, just beyond the PETROL STATION in **Magazia** (and opposite **Ag Spiridon**), turn left on a minor tarmac road signposted to BOITATIKA and AG APOSTOLI. The road becomes concrete, and in a little over 10 minutes you're in **Boitatika**. At a junction of concrete lanes, turn right between houses at the sign for AG APOSTOLI and SUNSET TAVERNA.

The little church of **Ag Apostoli (50min)** stands on a hillock, shaded by cypress trees — a wonderful place to take advantage of the magnificent vista over the Erimitis Cliffs, where the coastline rears up out of the azure sea into sheer chalky-coloured walls. In the churchyard a shaded table and benches offer an ideal picnic spot (Picnic 5). You can spend hours here contemplating the tremendous view shown on pages 22-23 and, if you are thirsty, the Sunset Bar is next to the church. Those who are not in a hurry and would like to spend more time in this area, may wish to venture down towards Pounda Point.*

Detour to Pounda Point (45min) _____

With the entrance to Sunset Bar behind you, cross their large car park and follow the stony track (part of a one-way traffic system) on the right. Turn left along another track and, in two minutes, turn right on a concrete lane leading towards·the headland. The lane reverts to stone and narrows to a path outside the gates of a small villa on the right. From this point on, there are magnificent views

into Achai Bay. A small sandy cove nestles at the foot of a half-moon of cliffs. Further down, you can see the Stakhes Caves, shown in the photograph. As you descend, the path steepens, becomes more bouldery, and is hemmed in by *maquis*. Nearing the point, a rope handrail assists your descent. If you decide to go down, take great care on the loose scree. If this seems too dangerous, and you feel too far from help, just stop to enjoy the views, before heading back up the hillside.

Three cloistered caves open out from the sea cliffs sheltering Achai Bay. This viewpoint is not far below the setting for Picnic 5.

The main walk does not visit Pounda; instead, leave the church (or bar) and walk back to the junction of concrete lanes, two minutes back, then return to the main road in **Magazia** (**1h15min**). *(Short walk 1 ends in this village and Short walk 2 begins here.)* Head north towards LAKKA, passing a shop and a bar a couple of minutes along. Leaving Magazia, turn left just past an old SCHOOL building on a minor tarmac road signposted to MANESATIKA and KASTANIDA. Pass a concrete lane climbing up by a stone wall on the left and, strolling along, just soak up the peacefulness of this sylvan countryside — the stillness being broken only by the bray of a donkey or the phutt-phutt of a passing motor scooter.

Just over 10 minutes along, in **Mitsialatika**, turn left at a concreted fork, following the signpost to KASTANIDA and SUNSET TAVERNA (a different Sunset Taverna!). Pass the church of **St Nicholas** on the left, followed by a tiny shop on your right (so small you may not even notice it). There is still an air of abandonment hanging over these small hamlets, and some houses are closed up, but there are also signs of houses being restored and walls rebuilt.

Continue along the concrete lane, ignoring another lane off left, until you reach signs for 'SUNSET'. This five-minute diversion leads you along a red-waymarked path to the left, passing through scrubby woodland. Suddenly you arrive at an eagle's nest VIEWPOINT on the cliff-edge, with a dizzying drop down to the seething sea below. *Keep clear of the edge and beware of vertigo!*

Return to the concrete lane and turn left. Follow the lane downhill, ignoring a lane off to the left. Half a minute later, the land ends at an untidy farm dwelling, but you continue along a walled path at the left-hand side of the building. This lovely, shady path swings right and then left before passing the small chapel of **Ag Isayros** on the left. There are two derelict stone buildings opposite. A minute below the chapel, the path joins a stony track at a T-junction. Turn right. *Attention!* Only 20m/yds down the track, be careful to turn right on a steeply descending mule track with a wall on the left (a small stone cairn *may* indicate the start of this path). The path drops down into a heavily wooded valley via some steep zigzags. Just below these you join a level path crossing your route, built along a terrace. Through the trees you may catch sight of the tall campanile of Ipapanti church.

Turn right on this path, which descends in broad steps to a small concrete FOOTBRIDGE over a stream bed. Just off to the right is **Ipapanti Spring**, sometimes called 'Circe's Spring', after the woman who trapped Odysseus, turning his men into pigs. Climb the path beyond the bridge, below a high retaining wall, to reach **Ipapanti Church**. This is the only Byzantine church on Paxos and was once a bishop's seat. You arrive at the foot of the tall belfry shown below (see also Walk 7 and photograph on page 16), a very peaceful spot, with ample shade. If the door to the belfry is open, climb to the top to enjoy an unrivalled view over the olive groves to Lakka and beyond, to Corfu.

With the CAMPANILE and adjoining steps on your right, continue the walk by heading along an alley between houses. In a minute, where a concrete lane zigzags down to the left, bear right along a path by a wall, reaching another concrete lane in half a minute. Turn left down this lane, passing a fine Venetian stone archway leading to an impressive stone manor house above to your right. Follow the concrete lane as it twists downhill through olive groves and, 20 minutes after leaving the church belfry, you reach the main road to Lakka. Turn left, and in another 20 minutes you come to the placid waters of the harbour at **Lakka** (**2h 30min**).

The elegant campanile of Ipapanti Church, visited in both Walk 5 and Walk 7.

6 LOGGOS TO LAKKA (VIA THE COAST)

See also photographs pages 4-5, 20, 43

Distance: 5.8km/3.6mi; 3h

Grade: moderate to strenuous, with plenty of ups and downs. Recommended only for fit walkers, and *not recommended in wet weather*.

Equipment: sturdy shoes or walking boots, sunhat, suncream, long-sleeved shirt, long trousers, cardigan, rainwear, bathing suit, picnic, water

How to get there: 🚌 to Loggos
To return: 🚌 from Lakka

Short walks

1 Loggos — Glyfada Beach — Loggos: 1h15min; moderate, with steep ascents and descents; 🚌 to and from Loggos. *Not recommended for young children, and dangerous in wet conditions.* Glyfada Beach is only accessible on foot or by sea. Follow the main walk to Glyfada and return the same way.

2 Lakka — Orkos Beach — Lakka: 1h10min; easy; 🚌 to and from Lakka. Walk out of Lakka on the bus road. After 0.8km (half a mile), at a steep hairpin bend, take the second of two concreted lanes dipping off to the left. This lane runs close to the main road for a short time. At a fork, with many villa signs, turn left. After about 80m/yds look for a path on your right leading down into the valley. This is the beginning of a 20-minute walk to Orkos Beach — a beautiful shady walk which crosses the valley floor further down and emerges by the cluster of round huts which can be seen from the sea. Return the same way, or follow the main walk route back to Lakka (notes begin on page 52).

The idyllic little coves that lie scattered along the east coast make this island the gem that it is. They warrant a cove crawl, and this hike is the second half of it (the first half being Walk 4). By boat it will cost you much less energy; by foot you pay with a couple of hours and possibly a blister, but the reward certainly outshines the discomfort. Don't forget your suncream!

Begin the walk in **Loggos**; take the broad path behind the old soap factory — the BUILDING WITH THE TALL CHIMNEY, on the left-hand side of the port (as you face the sea). A few yards uphill, beyond the factory chimney, leave the path (which only goes to the building ahead) and take a flight of steps on your left. Almost immediately turn up right on a path, which offers some splendid views across the harbour as it twists uphill. In a few minutes you come to the foot of a DERELICT WINDMILL that crowns the promontory hilltop (Picnic 6). From here you have the excellent view over Loggos shown on pages 4-5. The pastel-coloured village stands just on the waterfront; olive-

48

After your visit to Monadentri cove, cooled off and ready for another breath-consuming ascent, find a clear path near the far end of the beach, which climbs a bank and disappears into a sea of heather — a beautiful sight in autumn, when the hillside is a mass of pink flowers.

clad hills cascade down around it. It's picture-postcard perfect. If you climb the old mill walls for your view, *do so with the utmost care.*

Continuing on, now swing left, following the garden wall you have been circling (on your left). Ignore the path to the right here, descending steeply to a tiny cove. Barely a minute further along, you enjoy the uninterrupted view along the coast seen in the photograph on page 52, with its striking colour contrasts of dark green inclines, limestone-grey shoreline, and royal blue sea. The limestone shelf can be reached via a path off to the right here.

Further along the wall, you'll see the remains of a SECOND WINDMILL on your left. The belfry piercing the cape of olive trees, over on the right, is your immediate target. You soon pass a narrow alley forking off to the left. (You could return to Loggos this way, if you just want a very short walk.) Keeping straight on, you reach a track on the outskirts of **Dendiatika**. Pass a concrete lane coming up steeply from the right. *Attention!* Just 30m/yds beyond this lane, turn right on a path at the corner of a chain-link fence. Follow it through the olive trees to reach a concrete lane; ANTIGONE APARTMENTS are immediately opposite. Take the alley on the left-hand side of them, for the next section of the walk — down to Glyfada Bay. (You can also return to Loggos from here: turn left and then left again at the next junction.) Beyond the apartments the alley turns right and then left, above a LARGE SWIMMING POOL. It continues between high stone walls, with a stunning view through olive and cypress trees to the sea below. After a short uphill section, turn downhill at a fork. Watch your step from now on, as you plunge and corkscrew downhill to the **Glyfada Beach** (**45min**). The swimming is superb, and

on the far side of the beach are limestone slabs for sunbathing. It is a favourite beach for naturists.

Unfortunately, it is no longer possible to walk around the coast from Glyfada to Monadentri Beach; the path has been fenced off, and we have to head inland for a while. Having stopped for a picnic or swim, make

Sternbergia on the shady hillside above Monadentri Beach

your way to the far side of the beach, following a path just above. At the end of the beach, pick up a rough path heading inland (there is a wall and fence on the right). Ascend the path through a wooded valley and, in five minutes, you emerge on a lane at the gated entrance to GLYFADA BEACH VILLAS on your right. Follow the lane as it winds uphill and, at the top of the hill (six minutes up), turn right at a T-junction on a tarmac road. You shortly pass the small church of **Ag Dimitrios** on the left. One minute later, where the road bears left, turn right on a walled footpath, which soon steepens as it climbs through woodland. Two minutes along this path, with some rocky steps ahead, turn right on a pretty, level path which

Agave americana (Century plant)

continues along a terrace. This path may be slightly overgrown, but in another three minutes you will take the next left turn — just before a block of apartments. Keep this building and its wall on your right, to meet a concrete lane. Turn right, and meet the MAIN ROAD TO LAKKA in another two minutes.

Turn right on the main road and, two minutes later, at the chapel of **Ag Spiridon**, turn right again, on a wide descending track. The next section of the walk takes you down to **Monadentri Beach (1h30min)**, a fine long bay with two bars where you can quench your thirst. Have a swim and take a rest, to prepare for the next part of the walk — a steep climb up to the scattered little hamlets between Loggos and Lakka.

This climb begins near the far end of the beach. Turn up the bed of a watercourse and in 20m/yds, pick up a steep path on the right, to reach a track below a TAVERNA WITH SEVERAL WALLED TERRACES. Cross the track and take the path opposite — notice the WHITE-PAINTED ROCKS edging the path. This path (shown on page 49) is beautiful sight in autumn, when the hillside is a mass of pink flowers.

Splashes of blue and red paint guide you along through the flowering shrubs and cypresses. Ignoring a path going left, enter olive groves and walk through them to a concrete lane. Follow this lane ahead until you reach a junction, where you turn right, steeply

Picnic 6: Climb the promontory above Loggos for this superb view of the limestone shelves edging the coastline.

downhill, on another concrete lane signed to LAKKOS BEACH. The lane descends ever more steeply until, at the entrance to **Villa Anassa**, you drop down a flight of concrete steps on the left and descend a short, rocky path to the beach. **Lakkos Beach (2h)**, a pebbly cove set in the shadows of a darkly wooded hillside, is usually deserted. There is supposed to be a path back uphill from the north end of the beach, but unless you are equipped for mountaineering on loose scree, it is more prudent to return up the concrete lane.

When you reach the 'LAKKOS BEACH' SIGN at the top of the hill again, continue straight ahead along the lane. Do *not* turn left at a junction five minutes later. The concrete changes to tarmac, and you reach a road junction in another five minutes (with a single-storey house on the right). Turn right along another narrow tarmac road and, 80m/yds further on, turn right on a footpath signposted to ORKOS BEACH.

This is one of the most delightful paths on the island and runs downhill through a 'glen', with a stream bed on your right. When alight with spring or autumn flowers, it looks like an illustration for a book of fairytales. Crossing the stream bed halfway down, 15 minutes after leaving the road, you pass to the right of the JUVENTAS ENCLOSURE WITH ITS RONDAVEL HUTS, and

Some other flowers you might see on Paxos (from top to bottom): Anacamptis pyramidalis (pyramidal orchid), Ranunculus, anemone, and Urginea maritima (sea squill)

reach **Orkos Beach** (**2h30min**), perhaps one of the loveliest on Paxos.

When you are ready to leave, go along the beach and turn left after passing the ROUND STONE BUILDING, then swing right after a few metres. Two branches on the right lead to private villas — keep to the main path, which runs below a wall, through a pine wood. *Attention!* Arriving at a Y-fork, bear right, uphill, onto a higher path at the corner of the wall; do *not* go straight ahead on the lower, level path which has a low wall on its left. Now climb more steeply, with a wall and barbed wire close by on the right. At the top of the wall, bear right, to follow the wall along a narrow and perhaps overgrown, level path. In two minutes you reach a concrete lane and turn left uphill.*

The concrete lane takes you up to a tarmac road after 50m/yds. Here turn right on another concrete lane signed to villas PANORAMA, NINA and ANGEL-LOW. In 100m/yds, turn left at VILLA NINA, then follow the unsurfaced, walled track round a right-angled bend and join the top end of another concrete lane. Turn left here. The lane descends ever-more steeply through olive groves. Five minutes after joining this lane (after rounding a couple of very steep zigzag bends), you reach the waterfront at **Lakka** (**3h**).

*But if you want to visit another beach, turn right downhill: after 100m/yds take a narrow, signed path on the left. This descends through woodland to the rocky cove of Arkoudaki. The narrow path continues round the coast, becoming easier to follow as it turns the headland, passing close to a light beacon, before reaching Lakka.

53

7 LAKKA • CAPE LAKKA • VASSILATIKA • IPAPANTI CHURCH • LAKKA

See also photographs pages 16, 20, 47

Distance: 7.5km/4.7mi; 3h20min

Grade: moderate to strenuous for less experienced walkers, with some (short) rough stretches en route.

Equipment: sturdy shoes or walking boots, sunhat, suncream, long-sleeved shirt, long trousers, cardigan, rainwear, bathing suit, picnic, water

How to get there: 🚐 to Lakka
To return: 🚐 from Lakka

Short walks

1 Lakka — Plani Beach — Lakka: 1h30min; easy, but involves some scrambling through hillside scrub and a few short ascents and descents; access/return as above. Follow the main walk up to the concrete lane swinging round in front of you (the 50min-point). Here keep left and descend to Lakka, remaining on the lane. (Take care around the 'rock tables' near Plani Beach, where the path is in danger of crumbling away.)

2 Lakka — reservoir — Lakka: 1h40min; fairly easy; access/return as above. Follow the main walk to the roadside shrine of Ag Fotini (1h25min). One minute after passing this shrine, on an uphill section of concrete in front of a cottage, turn left on a stepped path. This path, between walls, takes you down into a delightfully cool and shady valley. Two minutes down the path you reach a track with the restored church of Ag Ioannis on the left. Follow the track around to the back of the church and continue downhill; a sign points to 'Reservoir–Lakka'. After five minutes you arrive at a bowl-shaped reservoir, usually nearly empty. Follow the lane round the reservoir, on either side, to reach another track. Follow this down to the Lakka road and head left, back to Lakka.

Explore Cape (Akr) Lakka and discover a variety of beaches and seascapes. Then move on to the plunging escarpment of the west coast, an inaccessible wall of cliffs that will leave you in awe. Inland, the countryside is a timeless masterpiece. Enchanting old lanes lead you through the Paxos of centuries ago … and the Paxos of today — there is little difference between the two.

Start the walk in **Lakka**: take the steps up between the last two restaurants at the western end of the PORT. You pass below a CHURCH and then continue around the coastline to two beaches, both of which are wonderful for children.

Straight off the end of the second beach, head up into thick scrub, following a well-used path that climbs the face of the hill. In three minutes you reach the headland track with an apartment building on your right. Turn right along the track. From the TOP OF THE RIDGE here on **Cape Lakka** you have a magnificent panorama over the beautiful crystal-clear waters of the harbour. You might like to stop here for Picnic 7a, in the setting shown on page 20. Looking across the northern side of the enclosing arm, you see Corfu, from the white cliffs of the south to the hilly west coast. A few minutes along the crest, the track ends at a 'NO SHOOTING' SIGN. Two paths lead off from here. First take the one straight ahead; it descends through woodland to an isthmus just south of Cape Lakka, with two small beaches, one either side of the headland. Return to the end of the track and take the other path, now on your right. Follow it down through *maquis* into a shallow valley. The path swings right

Close on 30 minutes from Lakka, we slide down onto isolated Plani Beach, where curious rock 'tables' jut out into the sea.

alongside a stream bed and leads you to the rocky cove shown below, **Missorachi Beach (30min)**. It's backed by impressive cliffs, and the water is an inviting turquoise-green — but note that the sea can be quite rough on this side of the point.

Returning to the ridge track, head uphill towards the lighthouse. At the crest of the hill, a pine wood offers welcome shade. At the top, turn right at a track junction, to visit the LIGHTHOUSE (**45min**). Below the lighthouse, to the left, is an unusual beach known as 'Plani'. To get there, head back from the lighthouse, passing your outward track on the left. After 100m/yds, turn sharp right down another stony track. This track has obliterated the original footpath down to the coast, but it is an easy zigzag descent and, in less than 10 minutes you will reach isolated **Plani Beach (1h)** and an emerald-green bay. Around the corner to the left, curious limestone 'tables' jut out into the sea. Cliffs tower in the background. If you decide to walk around on these rock 'tables', go *carefully*; they are slippery and crumbly. You can continue around the shelf for another three minutes or so, for the beautiful view of the sea caves and cove shown on page 55.

Return to the intersection where you turned off for the lighthouse but, this time, keep straight on — until you reach a concrete lane swinging round in front of you, three minutes up. Follow this lane up to the right. *(But those of you doing Short walk 1 descend to the left here.)* Wandering amidst these peaceful sylvan hills you head through **Dalietatika** — a shy sprinkling of cottages set back in the trees. The houses become more dispersed and the countryside 'friendlier'.

The lane from Dalietatika to Vassiliatika is now mostly a concrete road, but is is still one of the most enjoyable easy walks on Paxos. The pretty valley leading down to Lakka is visible most of the way. The lane soon takes you between two country churches, **Ag Vasilios** and **Ag Dimitrios**. Continue gently uphill until you pass a roadside SHRINE on the left dedicated to **Ag Fotini** (**1h25min**). *(Short walk 2 turns left one minute after passing this little shrine.)* The main walk continues along the concrete here, soon passing a track junction.

The lane steepens as it enters the hamlet of **Vassiliatika** and becomes mossy under the trees. As the lane swings to the right uphill you see facing you a fine VENETIAN MANOR linked with occupied houses on the left. Make a short diversion here by passing through the arch, climbing the steps and turning right along a walled path directly in front of the manor house. Take care along the path, because the walls are collapsing in places. In just two minutes you come out in open coastal *maquis.* Turn left at the end of the wall, and a few steps will being you to a magnificent VIEWPOINT overlooking the west coast — another superb, peaceful picnic setting.

To continue the walk, return to the archway and turn right. Follow the shady path between walls as it gently climbs the hill and then, after passing through a spinney, joins a rather overgrown track. Continue ahead along the track and, where it swings off to the left, take the path straight ahead. Be aware that you are now near the edge of a high precipice. Only a metre/yard over to your right, you're looking straight down into a keyhole-shaped chasm that slices inland from the sea. What a sight! An exhilarating, but rather frightening, lookout point! Don't venture too near the edge. The path, littered with shotgun cartridges, continues uphill, never far from the edge of the gaping inlet on the right. (If you find this path too

Missorachi Beach, one of the settings for Picnic 7a

vertiginous, stay on the track.) A ruined windmill peers above the juniper bushes on the hilltop ahead.

Having circled the inlet, the path runs alongside a wall on the left and joins a concrete lane. Turn left downhill, in one minute reaching a THREE-WAY JUNCTION. Go down the middle branch and, in three minutes, look out for a walled path joining from the right. This is where Walk 5 joins us for the rest of the walk. (You might like to spend a few minutes exploring this shaded path with the small chapel of Ag Isayros on the right.)

Attention is needed here! Just 20m/yds along the track beyond the path junction, turn right on a steeply descending mule path with a wall on the left (it may be marked with a small stone cairn). The path drops down into a heavily wooded valley via some steep zigzags. Just below these you join a level path crossing your route, built along a terrace. Through the trees you may catch sight of a tall campanile. Turn right on this path to reach **Ipapanti Church** (**2h35min**; see page 47). The bright ochre façade of this Byzantine church (see page 16) cheers up this dark corner of the valley. Ipapanti (Picnic 7b) is the oldest church on the island (see page 21) and unique for its two circular rooftop domes. Unfortunately it is kept locked. One of the few springs on the island (**Ipapanti Spring**) is found in the little gulley you crossed, behind the church. It's a lush spot. The path is flooded with cyclamen in autumn. Not a sound can be heard in Grammatikeika, the village above. The picnic spot is not only a beautiful setting, but it has also been suggested by Tim Severin in *The Ulysses Voyage* (Hutchinson, 1987) that the Ipapanti spring and glade was the scene of Ulysses' encounter with Circe, the sylvan goddess of the golden hair. Circe turned his sailors into swine, but it all turned out well in the end and Ulysses was beguiled into a year's stay. It really does sound just like Paxos...

Now, using the notes for Walk 5 on page 47, second paragraph, return to **Lakka** (**3h20min**).

8 AROUND ANTIPAXOS

Distance: 7.5km/4.7mi; 3h

Grade: moderate, with a steady 15-minute ascent at the outset. *Not recommended in wet weather*, when the tracks get very muddy.

Equipment: sturdy shoes, sunhat, suncream, long-sleeved shirt, long trousers, cardigan, rainwear, bathing suit, picnic, water

How to get there: 🚤 During the season taxi boats leave from Gaios for Vrika and Voutoumi between 10.00 and 12.00. There is also the odd boat from Lakka and Loggos.

To return: 🚤 The last boats leave the beaches at 17.00. Always verify the last boat back; departure times may change!

Short walks

1 Vrika — Vigla — Voutoumi Beach — Vrika: 1h; grade, access/return as above. This walk shows you a good cross-section of the island with the minimum of effort. Follow the main walk as far as the concrete lane descending to Agrapidia (the 25min-point). Then pick up the notes at the 2h20min-point and follow the walk to the end.

2 Vrika — Vigla — Agrapidia — Voutoumi Beach — Vrika: 1h50min; grade, access/return as above. Do the main walk, but exclude the lighthouse detour, by keeping right at the intersection reached in 1h.

Note: There are two tavernas on Vrika Beach and another high above Voutoumi Beach.

Most holiday-makers on Paxos make a day trip to Antipaxos — word quickly gets around about the island's sandy beaches. Few people, however, venture beyond these beaches, and most tourists remain unaware that this speck in the sea (only

Voutoumi Bay, one of the settings for Walk 8 and Picnic 8, is considered by many to be the most beautiful beach in all of Greece.

3 sq km!) has more to offer than sand and sea. Less than 15 minutes uphill from Vrika (where the taxi boats land) the salubrious tangle of vineyards and garden plots shown opposite awaits you. Cobbled alleys criss-cross the island's hump like a great maze, connecting the farm dwellings that dot the landscape. Do the island justice — go out for a stroll.

Leave the boat at the small cove of **Vrika** and **start the walk**. At the far end of the beach, head up the rough track that climbs towards VIGLA. A minute up, you pass a track off to the left, which leads to another cove (Messovrika). The slopes are thickly woven in the ubiquitous *maquis*. We have a fine view over Paxos, to Corfu and mainland Greece.

After passing below a vineyard, the track turns back towards the coast and you meet the MAIN TRACK FROM VOUTOUMI. Turn sharp right and continue uphill. *(But keep ahead along the main track to reach Voutoumi Beach — one of the settings for Picnic 8.)* A surprise awaits you as you mount the island's 'hump' — quite a substantial settlement of vineyards and gardens covers the crest. At the top of the track, pass between two houses and, just beyond them, turn left at a track junction; *don't* keep straight on. Old stone walls line the track and enclose the gardens.

You pass by the shuttered stone houses of **Vigla**, with their trellised courtyards. When it's grape-picking time, the island becomes a hive of activity, and the musky odour of crushed grapes permeates the air. Face-lifted cottages (and even some new houses) suggest that the 20the century has finally arrived here on Antipaxos as well. If you're not pressed for time, do some exploring, wander up some of the many side-alleys off the main route. Looking over the vineyards below you, the turquoise blue waters off Voutoumi Beach steal your attention with their alluring brightness. This beach, one of the finest in Greece, is the beauty spot of Antipaxos.The hills of Epirus rise in the background.

Nearly 10 minutes from the junction (**30min**), you join a concrete lane to the little port of Agrapidia and pass a fork off to the right (your return route from the lighthouse). Descending this lane, you look straight across onto the impressive northwest coast of Greece. Some 30m/yds down the lane, a track branches off to the left — your ongoing route to Voutoumi, when you return from the lighthouse. *(Short walk 1 turns left here.)*

Soon you're down in the sheltered little port of **Agrapidia** (**45min**), with boats moored to a jetty and others drawn up on the beach. Now follow the concrete lane straight ahead: a steep climb which returns you to gardens and vineyards. Notice the absence of olive trees on this island. After a hot 10-minute climb,

Looking out over vineyards, the turquoise blue waters off Voutoumi Beach steal your attention with their alluring brightness.

you pass a house on your right set behind an ugly concrete wall topped with broken glass and rusty barbed wire. Turn left onto another track between walls, opposite the gateway to this house. *(But for Short walk 2, continue straight ahead, following the concrete lane as it twists between garden walls and, when it joins a track, turn right.)*

Just over a minute along, where the track swings left, turn right on a narrow, stony path squeezed between walls. Follow the path down into a shallow valley and then uphill past a walled-in garden and a COTTAGE WITH BLUE SHUTTERS on the left (**1h**). At the top of the incline, turn left along the track which will take you to the lighthouse.

As you follow the track south, the countryside becomes less cultivated, less walled-in, and more open, with *maquis,* gorse, myrtle and other aromatic plants lining the route. Soon after passing some isolated small cottages set in vineyards, the landscape resembles a heath, and you see the limestone islets of Dasskalia off to the right. More of the Ionian islands lie in the distance. Passing through a grove of pine and cypress trees, you reach the LIGHTHOUSE (**1h 25min**). Circle it to the right and from the front gate, take a pathway leading down through a shady avenue of pines. The path curves left and comes to a small concrete jetty. A little cove beckons nearby on the left, but to get there you would have a difficult scramble over large rocks and you would need to paddle part of the way. Alternatively, you can swim off the jetty in deep clear water, but mind the sea urchins. From this jetty you can just make out Theotakos Monastery in the distance, on Panayia Island outside the northern entrance to Gaios harbour. The soft bed of needles and deep shade of the pines below the lighthouse make for a delightful picnic spot.

When you've had your fill of sun and solitude, return to the intersection where you turned off for the lighthouse (next to the cottage with blue shutters, about 25 minutes back) but, this time, head straight on into the profusion of walls and gardens. Keep ahead when you join the concrete track coming up from the right (from the port of Agrapidia). The track soon narrows, and you pass another track descending to the port. Follow a concrete path ahead, between walls. In a labyrinth of alleys, remain on the main